NADIA BAILEY

Illustrations by Phil Constantinesco

the book of
Barb

Smith Street Books

Contents

Welcome to the Book of Barb.

Barbara Holland appears in just four episodes of *Stranger Things*, and in one of those episodes, she's dead. She is, in the grand mythology of the series, a minor player: Nancy's awkward best friend, sacrificed early to give the heroes of the story the push they need to begin their quest.

We first meet her sauntering down the hallway of Hawkins High. She's tall with a swoop of red hair, large glasses, mom jeans, and a high-necked plaid blouse. She has freckles and wears sensible shoes. She's jazzed to know if Nancy's crush called. She pokes gentle fun when Nancy tries to downplay her blossoming relationship with Steve. She can read Nancy like a book.

There's an easy intimacy between them. They're probably best friends from childhood — same elementary school, same after-school activities (ballet first, until Barb got too tall, then music classes, debating, the school magazine) and same awkward teenage phase (except Nancy hides it better). They're in competition with each other in the way that all best friends are. And they're in love with each other the way best friends are, too.

Neither Nancy or Barb them has ever been cool, but Nancy has a chance. Adolescence has been kind to her. She's pretty and petite and she's caught the eye of the popular boy. She wants desperately to be liked and Steve is her way in.

You're gonna be so cool now, says Barb. You can hear it in her voice, that undercurrent of longing and fear. *You better still hang out with me, that's all I'm saying.* Barb will never be part of the Carol and Tommy H crowd. She'll never take off her spectacles and be suddenly, unexpectedly beautiful. When she takes off her glasses, she's still the same old Barb.

We all wanted to be Nancy growing up. Smart, pretty, likeable, caught between the affections of a popular jock and an alluringly artistic loner. Of course we wanted to be the one who looks cute while shotgunning a beer and gets to sleep with Steve Harrington at a Tuesday night pool party when his parents are out of town. But in reality, we were the ones whose attempts to be cool are more likely to end with us slicing our thumbs open. Who miss the electric moment when everyone else jumps in the pool. Who ends up sitting outside alone and lonely while our best friend is upstairs getting to third base. The one who gets taken, literally or figuratively, by a Demogorgon.

Deep down, we are all Barb.

We were the ones at the far periphery of the teenage social hierarchy, caught somewhere between being regarded as a brain (if we were lucky) or a loser (if we were not lucky). Nancy might be the girl we fantasised about being, but Barb — poor, sweet, misfit Barb — is who we were. And no matter how many years it's been since we left high school, no matter how much we tell ourselves that the cruelty of our teenage peers doesn't matter, not now, not after all these years, that's who we'll always be at heart.

In a world where Nancy is reinventing herself to be someone who Steve might like, Barb takes a stand to keep being herself. Nancy wants to be liked, to be accepted, to be approved of, but Barb truly doesn't care what people like Tommy H and Carol think about her. That's the secret of why Barb is cool: cool girls do not fret about whether they are cool; they don't care about being cool, and that is what makes them even cooler. She is secure in herself. It's only through her loyalty to Nancy that she's swayed to do anything she doesn't want to.

In the grand scheme of *Stranger Things*, Barb is a footnote. When Will goes missing, the whole town is in uproar. When Barb disappears, no one but Nancy seems to notice her absence. She's there, and then she's gone, little more than a blip in a world of telekinetic orphans and killer inter-dimensional monsters.

Barb's great tragedy is that she had so much potential. Imagine how her life would have gone: high school wouldn't have been kind to her, but one day she'd graduate and leave Hawkins and find a life for herself that was entirely her own. We want to tell her — as we've told ourselves — that it gets better.

We want justice for Barb.

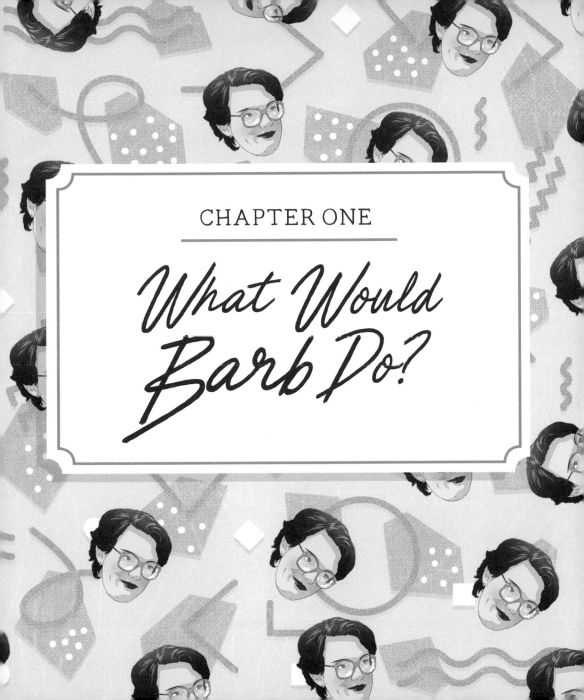

CHAPTER ONE

What Would Barb Do?

ASK
BARBARA

Got a problem
you can't solve?
Just chill.
Barb is here
to help.

Dear Barb,

My mom and dad split up a while back, and now my
dad lives with his new girlfriend.

He really doesn't care about me or my little brother
anymore, but my brother still idolises him and
thinks that one day he'll come back to us.

Should I tell my brother the truth or let him think
there's still hope?

I don't want to hurt him.

– Conflicted

Dear Conflicted,

It sounds like you're really close to your brother, and that's awesome.

But it's not up to you to tell him one way or the other what your dad is going to do in the future. After all, there's no way you can know that for sure (even if you think you do).

Instead, you should try to just be there for your brother, and let him know that no matter what happens, you'll never let him down. We all just want someone to care about us when we're hurt or scared or in trouble. Make sure your brother knows that you're there for him.

– Barb xox

Nance, seriously, you're gonna be so cool now, it's ridiculous.
You better still hang out with me, that's all I'm saying.

Which Hawkins High student are you?

Find out which Hawkins teen you most relate to with this handy quiz.

(Is it Barb? It's Barb, isn't it.)

1

Your teacher calls a surprise test. How do you feel?

a) You haven't studied, but, whatever. You really don't care if you pass or not.

b) You're nervous, but you'll be okay. You're smart. You've got this.

c) You've been preparing for this for weeks. A surprise? Please!

d) You're distracted with other things. Tests really aren't that important given everything else that's going on in your life.

2

What kind of music do you like to listen to?

a) Music is for nerds. You prefer sports.

b) You listen to the radio a lot — it's the best way to discover new bands.

c) You own every Blondie album.

d) The Clash, David Bowie, Television ... anything that's underground and kind of angsty.

3

A friend is in trouble. What do you do?

a) People tend to assume you'll flake, but actually you step up when it's needed.

b) Literally anything you can to help. You're very loyal.

c) Sometimes you're too wrapped up in your own life to be there for your friends. But you'll get around to it eventually.

d) You will resort to violence to defend your friends if necessary.

4

How would you describe your style?

a) Preppy. Money's no object so you always look good.

b) You've got your own thing going on. You're not interested in following trends.

c) You err on the side of conservative and you like things that are sweet and feminine.

d) You really don't care about clothes.

5

What's your vice?

a) Beer.

b) Caring too much.

c) Cute boys.

d) Voyeurism.

6

How's your social life going?

a) Bangin'. You're always hanging out with your friends, drinking, and throwing awesome parties when your parents are away.

b) You like to spend quality one-on-one time with your best friend.

c) You're really focussed on your grades right now. You'll see your friends once you're done studying.

d) Social life? What social life?

Mostly a) — You are *Steve*

You're confident, likeable and at the top of the social ladder. You have no problem landing dates or impressing your friends, although sometimes you let people influence you to do dumb things. You can come across as a bit of a jerk, but deep down you're actually a nice person who will come through in the end. Also, you have great hair.

Mostly b) — You are *Barb*

You're smart, wise and the best friend that anyone could have. You don't care much for the in-crowd — you always stay true to yourself rather than getting caught up in playing the popularity game. You're a quiet achiever who will one day go on to do great things. Don't worry. It gets better.

Mostly c) — You are *Nancy*

You're kind, clever and driven — once you decide you want something, you work hard to get it. While sometimes you can be a little bit insecure (you just want everyone to like you), you're also sensitive to other people's pain and hate injustice of any kind. Just make sure you remember who your true friends are.

Mostly d) — You are *Jonathan*

You're sensitive, artistic and a bit of a loner. You find it hard to open up to people, so you tend to just keep to yourself (or watch from a distance). If people think you're weird, that's their problem. You're very loyal to the few people you love and will fight for them no matter what the cost.

"We just made out a couple of times."

I told you, it's not like that.
Okay, I mean, yes, he likes me, but not like *that*.
We just made out a couple times.

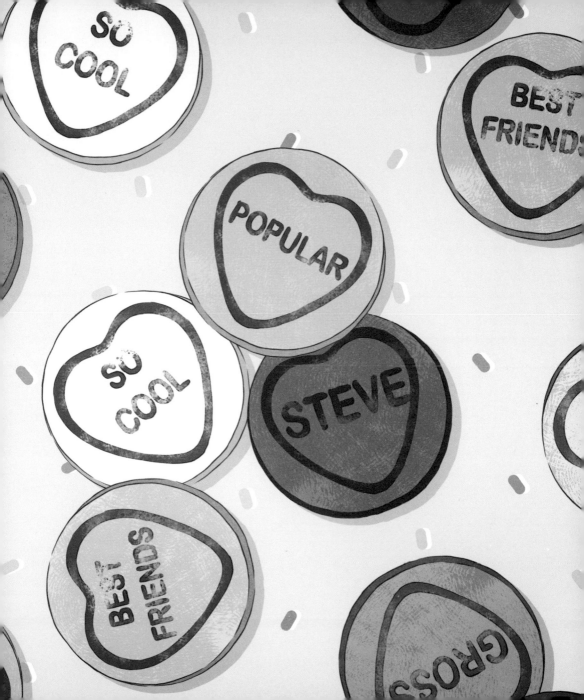

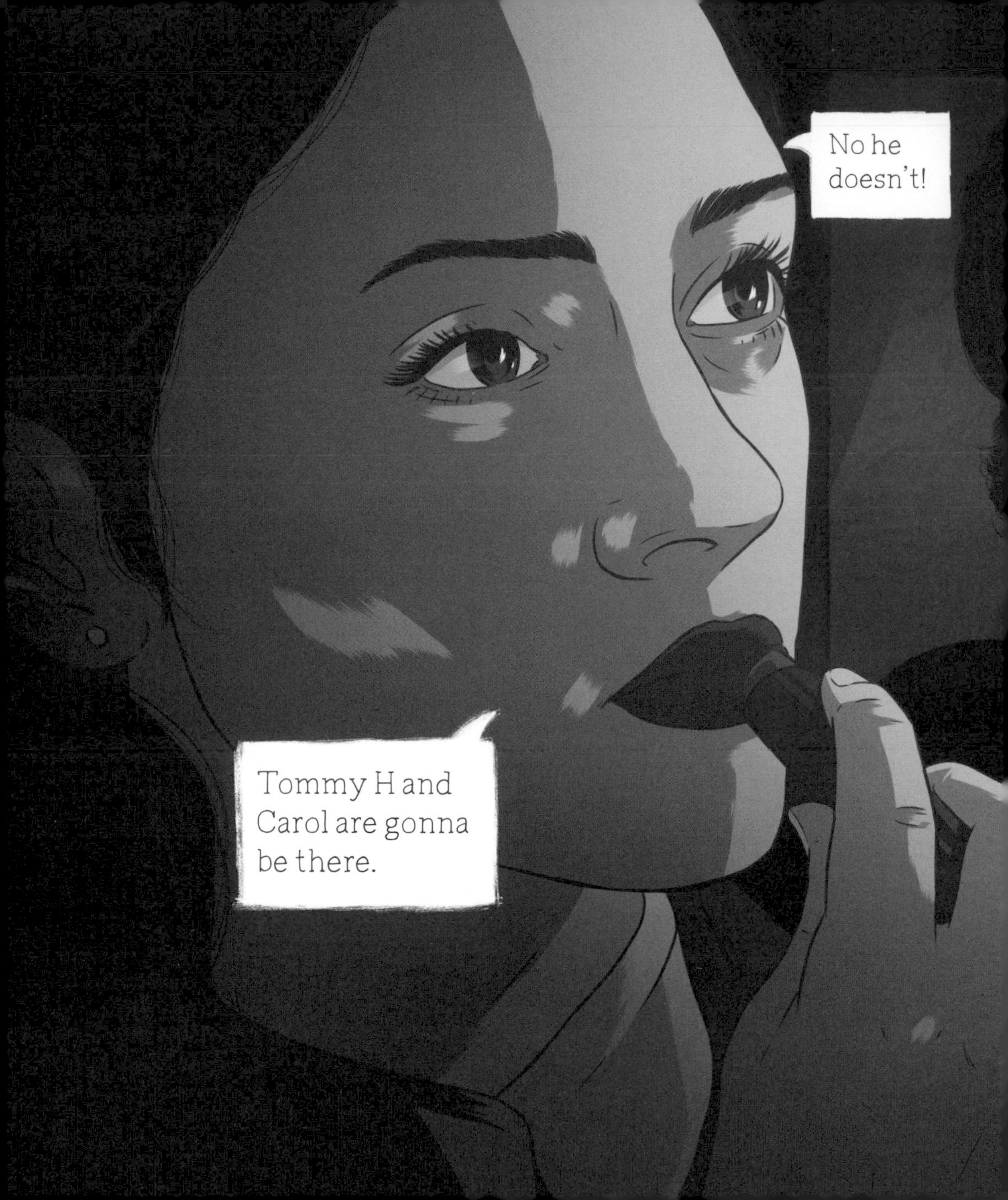
No he doesn't!
Tommy H and Carol are gonna be there.

He just wants to get in your pants.
Nance, seriously?
He invited you to his house. His parents aren't home.
Come on, you are not this stupid.
Tommy and Carol have been having sex since, like, seventh grade.
It'll probably just be, like, a big orgy.

Body Talk

Barb's Tips on Safe Sex

If your crush is looking to get you into bed, do yourself a favour and read this first.

Questions to ask yourself

Do you like him? Yes, but do you really like him? Does she like you? Does she make you feel good about yourself? Do they just want to get in your pants? Is he a perv? Will it be an orgy? Is that a new bra?

Don't do it for the wrong reasons

Just because Tommy H and Carol have been doing it since seventh grade, doesn't mean you have to. It's easy to compare yourself to other people and then feel bad about it. Don't do this! It's dumb, and it's just going to make you feel pressured to keep up with them or whatever. A good reason to have sex would be because you really want to and you really care about your partner. A bad reason would be because you care what people like Tommy H and Carol think.

Relationships take work

Okay, so there's more to being a couple than making out in the school bathrooms. Relationships take work. If someone really likes you, they'll show it in lots of little ways — by calling you up on the phone to talk for hours every night, or helping you study, or noticing when you've bought something new or changed your hair. If someone really loves you, they'll be there for you no matter what. Not just when things are easy, but when things are scary, too.

Keep a level head

Be smart and get educated. Go to Planned Parenthood and get information. Talk to them about contraception. You might want to get birth control pills or condoms (side note: do NOT rely on your crush to take care of this. If he or she doesn't have any condoms with them, make sure you do. You don't want to get caught out and wind up pregnant or with an STD). It's easy to get caught up in the moment so it's super important to think before you act.

Don't put up with double standards

Example: this guy – let's call him Steve – sleeps with Laurie, Amy and Becky. Everyone thinks that Laurie, Amy and Becky are sluts. But Steve? Nobody thinks any less of him. What's up with that? Don't let the person you're dating brand you as a slut just because you've dated other people. That kind of double standard is gross, and it's not okay. Remember: you are better than that.

ASK

BARBARA

Got a problem
you can't solve?
Just chill.
Barb is here
to help.

Dear Barb,

I'm in junior year and I'm worried about how I dress.

My parents never buy me new clothes – I have
to wear hand-me-downs from my older brothers that
are totally lame. At school, other kids tease me for
wearing old clothes.

How can I stop them laughing at me?

– Upset

Dear Upset,

First up, there's more to life than what the popular people think. What do they matter anyway? You can't stop them from being narrow-minded and petty, but you can choose to be around people who make you feel good about yourself. Even if you only have a couple of really good friends, if you stick with them, you'll always have someone to back you up. It's way easier to stand up for yourself when you have people who believe in you.

– Barb xox

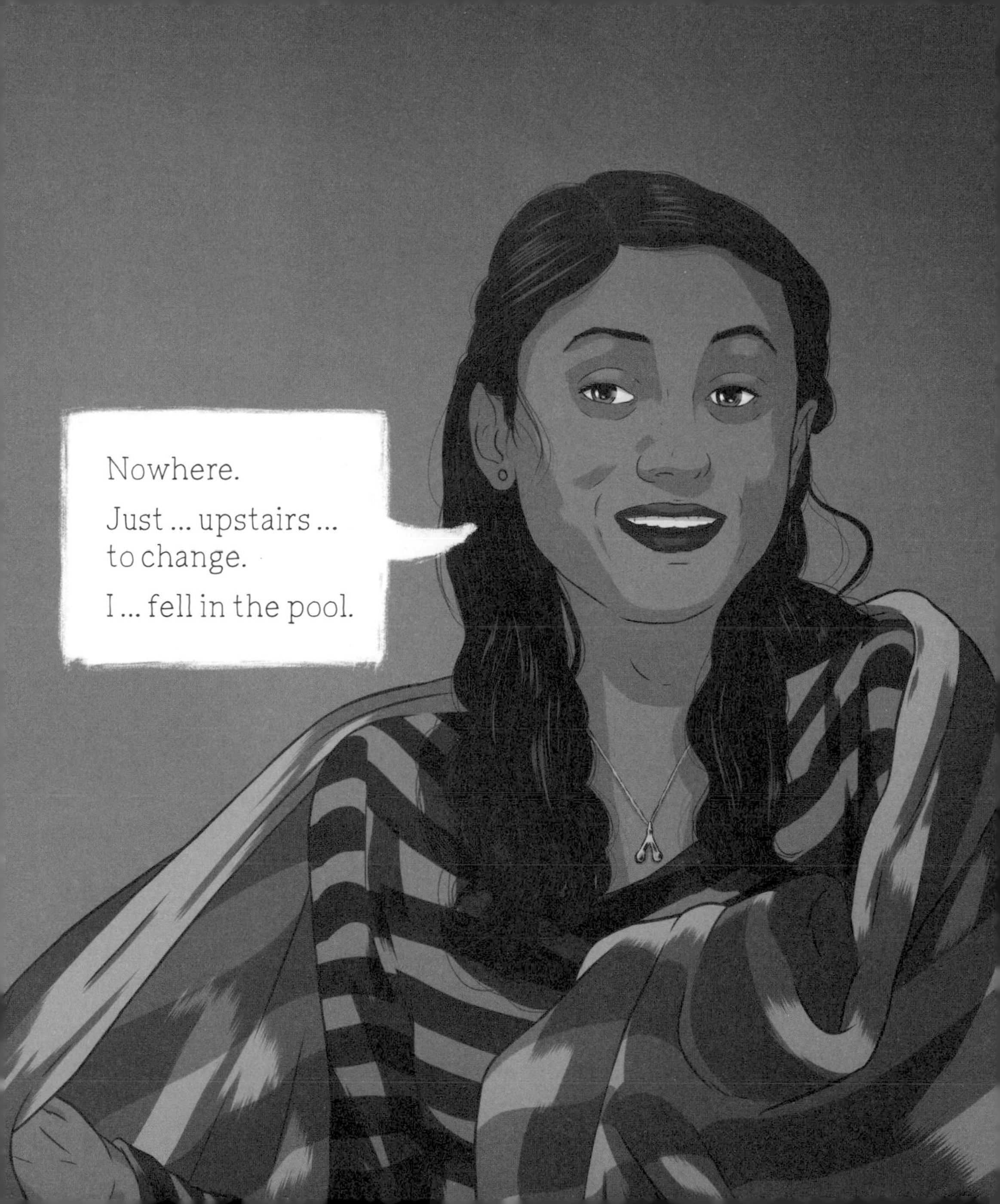
Nowhere.
Just ... upstairs ... to change.
I ... fell in the pool.

Why don't you just go ahead and go home? I'll just get a ride or something.
Barb ... I'm fine.

What's Your Sign

Your astrological reading for December, 1984.

Aries

Ride your bike at night.
Be on guard for people
who claim to be something
they're not. You will feel
elated, and then terrified.

Your power item: *a plaid ruffled top.*

Taurus

Find a way to talk about
your feelings. Drink Hershey's
Cocoa every morning for
a week. Reject doorways
into other worlds.

Your power item: *high-waisted jeans.*

Cancer

Experiment with a new look.
Realise that your sadness
is also your strength. Avoid
swimming pools at all costs.

Your power item: *ice-blue eyeshadow.*

Gemini

Don't be ruled by other
people's expectations.
Hang Christmas lights
in your loungeroom.
Indulge in a single vice.

Your power question: *"Is that a new bra?"*

Leo

Rearrange your life to
accommodate a new
friendship. Consider getting
drunk. Take a baseball bat
with you wherever you go.

Your power item: *great hair.*

Virgo

It's time to organise. Stand at the edge of a cliff and think about flying. Your friendship is only meaningful if it's accompanied by action.

Your power item: *a pink ruffled sweater.*

Libra

Stop for a moment and clear your head. Listen to 'Should I Stay or Should I Go?' by The Clash. Consider shoplifting something.

Your power item: *gold earrings.*

Scorpio

Your mood will improve if you keep mornings for coffee and contemplation. Avoid the woods. Think about a time you were happy.

Your power item: *a Schlitz beer.*

Sagittarius

You will experience a boost in popularity. Cultivate a healthy distrust in scientists. Reconnect with an old lover.

Your power item: *tan chinos.*

Capricorn

Imagine a world in which you are at peace. Let out your anger via telekinesis. Chew Bazooka bubble gum.

Your power phrase: *"I'm chill"*

Aquarius

Plan a new career path. Take an SLR camera everywhere you go. For luck, wear a gold necklace with a ballet slipper charm.

Your power item: *clear-framed glasses.*

Pisces

Whatever you're thinking about doing, don't. You are not this stupid. For peace, listen to Joy Division.

Your power item: *a blue puffer jacket.*

ASK BARBARA

Got a problem you can't solve? *Just chill.* Barb is here to help.

Dear Barb,

There's a boy I like but I don't know if he likes me.

When we're alone, he's really sweet, but he acts really differently when we're around his friends.

I think he might be embarrassed to be seen with me.

Do you have any advice?

– Confused

Dear Confused,

If a boy is a jerk to you, he isn't worth your time. Come on, you are not this stupid! Don't waste your time on someone who doesn't respect you, no matter how cute he is, or how much you like making out with him. If he really liked you, he would tell his friends that he's serious about you. You could try talking to him about his behaviour, but honestly?

You could do better.

– Barb xox

Barbara, pull over.
We can't park in the driveway.
The neighbours might see!

What? What are we doing here?
His house is three blocks away.
Are you serious?
This is so stupid.
I'm just gonna drop you off.

Barb's Party
Do's and Don'ts

No Parents. Big House. A Party?

Navigating the world of social gatherings can be tricky, especially in a town like Hawkins. Barb is here to help you get on the level.

Do

* Arrive with your best friend. It's weird and awkward to have to show up on your own, so double up with your BFF and you'll both feel better.

* Plan your outfit. If that means going shopping all weekend to find the perfect top, then so be it.

* Wear something you feel comfortable in. It doesn't have to be fancy. It could be as simple as putting on a jacket.

* Make a pact with your best friend. You are each other's guardian angels. It's your job to make sure they don't do anything stupid and they will do the same for you.

Don't

* Change who you are just to impress people. Seriously, you're better than that. Who cares what they think anyway?

* Cave to peer pressure. Just because everyone else is chugging beer and jumping in the pool, doesn't mean you have to.

* Let down your best friend. If they're about to do something stupid, be their guardian angel. Let your bestie know you're there for them.

* Go off on your own. It's not safe. Who knows what could happen?

CHAPTER TWO

The Secrets of Barb Style

Get the Look

Plaid World

In the stifling social arena where teens are pitted against each other in a never-ending quest for popularity (aka, high school), Barb does her own damn thing in classic separates.

Oversized statement frames: the ultimate style flex

This blouse says, 'I'm serious about school, but I also care about looking cute. Those things are not mutually exclusive, you know.'

Mom jeans: iconic

Comfortable shoes

The Barb 'Do

It's all about
the swoosh and roll.

Step 1

Start by grabbing your bottle of mousse. Squeeze out a palm-sized amount and work it through your hair until your locks feel a bit tacky. Tacky is good. That means the mousse is working.

Step 2

Using a comb, section your hair into a deep side part. Leave the top section as is for now; grab the bottom section and twist it towards your head until it forms a roll. Secure with bobby pins and give it a spray with some hairspray to keep it in place.

Step 3

Take the top section of your hair and spritz it all over with hairspray. Using your comb, tease it up until it gets nice and big. Remember: the higher the hair, the closer to God.

Step 4

Take your brush and gently smooth down your hair. Then take the top part and roll it towards your head on a hot roller. While you're waiting for it to set, take a break. Now would be a great time to call up your best friend, play Blondie's latest or get some study done.

Step 5

Gently remove the roller from your hair and brush it out until it forms a swoosh over your forehead. You may need to coax it into place. Once it's perfect, spray it again to set the look.

Step 6

You look great. Now, don't be late for class — you have a chemistry test this week and you're going to ace it.

Get the Look

Pretty in Pink

Sure, Nance has the girly thing down to a fine art, but Barb's take on femme is a masterclass in cool.

Watch and learn.

Matching
Trapper Keeper

Frilly without
being prissy

Cute watch

Barb's
getting-things-done
pants

Made for
walking
(not so good for
running away from
Demogorgons, though)

Brains before beauty

A Hawkins High Study Guide
by Barbara Holland

You could be forgiven for thinking that school is just one big popularity contest. I'm here to tell you it's not. Yes, having a social life is important, but doing well and getting good grades matter — especially if, like me, you're planning on going to college. So don't get caught out by a chemistry test or a tricky English paper — here are my tips for succeeding at school.

Make a study space

If your little brother insists on playing Dungeons & Dragons with his annoying friends while you're trying to cram for an algebra test, you're not going to get very far. Mark out a no-interruptions zone in your house — it could be your bedroom, or a spot in the basement, or even a quiet corner in the garage if you're really desperate. All the better if it's a really boring part of the house, where you can't be tempted to call up your best friend and moan about how hard studying is.

Team up

Having a study partner is a great way to make homework seem fun. If you're prepping for an exam, make a set of flash cards and then quiz each other. You'll remember heaps more if you practice out loud. Whatever you do, don't team up with your crush. It might seem like a cute way to spend time together and get work done, but trust me — it always ends in more making out and less studying.

Make lists

Because there's nothing more satisfying than crossing things off them.

Practise, practise, practise

Go through your flash cards. Then go through them again. Re-read your textbook. Get your best friend to test you using their flash cards too. I know it's boring, but you'll thank me when you get your marks back.

Reward yourself

If you're struggling with motivation, give yourself a reason to keep going. For example, make a deal with yourself that if you finish your practice test, you can go catch a film at the Hawk movie theatre. Or if you get through your reading, you can treat yourself to lunch at Benny's for a burger. It could even be something small: like, if you get through a round of flash cards without getting one wrong, you can call up your best friend to talk about your day. Whatever makes you feel happy.

That's it for now, Hawkins cohort. Good luck with your study!

A Field Guide to Eyewear in Hawkins

Be like Barb in a pair of iconic oversized frames, or take inspiration from other eyewear hits of the eighties.

The Barb

Needs no introduction. These are Barb's signature frames, guaranteed to make you feel at least 10 per cent sassier the moment you put them on.

The Wayfarer

Immortalised by Don Henley, and without a doubt what Steve would wear when he takes Nancy on a date to the park to 'study'.

The Ringwald

A strong choice for the fashion-conscious, best paired with a bucket hat, a pout and a love of the colour pink.

The Barb II

As seen in a snap of Barb and Nancy goofing off in a photo booth, these sunnies capture Barb's offbeat yet considered style.

The Dad Aviator

As seen on Mr Wheeler, these frames should be worn strictly by those over the age of 50. There's no way these will ever be cool.

Barb's Make-Up Secrets

True beauty is achieved when
you fully *own* your look.

That's what makes Barb's makeup so
special: she knows what works for her
and she executes it flawlessly.

Be like Barb. Wear what you like.

BLUE EYESHADOW.

Barb is so ahead of the curve with this one – blue is THE colour of the 80s.

BLUSH.

Barb wears a true pink that contrasts with the sweet copper tones of her freckles.

APRICOT SCRUB.

A no-fuss skincare regime that leaves Barb plenty of time to do more important things like make mixtapes or have endless phone convos with Nancy.

BLACK MASCARA.

Barb applies one, two or three coats depending on whether it's a school day, a weekend, or a party at Steve's house.

PINK LIPSTICK.

Barb wears a true pink – not a nude or a peach – to bring out her features to their best advantage.

FOUNDATION.

Barb favours a sheer foundation that doesn't hide her freckles – instead, they shine through like a tiny, lovely galaxy.

67

Put it On: Barb Beauty

To recreate Barb's look, all you need are a handful of products that you can literally buy anywhere.

But the DGAF attitude?

That's all up to you.

Start by washing your face and applying a generous scoop of apricot scrub to your skin. Now spend a few peaceful moments exfoliating in small, clockwise circles. Think about calling your best friend. Wash off the scrub with tepid water and pat dry.

Squeeze foundation onto the back of your hand and dot it gently onto your face using your fingertips. Blend, blend, blend. You want a light, sheer layer, not a mask. If you have freckles, let them shine. If you don't, DIY some using light-brown eyeliner pencil.

Pick out a blue eyeshadow. Note: Barb has brown eyes, so a light, shimmery blue looks great on her. Apply to your eyelids in layers to build up the colour and/or drama.

Grab your blush and sweep it across your cheekbones, focussing on the area closest to your temples for that, 'girl from a Robert Palmer video' vibe.

Apply a coat of mascara to your eyelashes. Wait for it to dry, then do a second coat. You want your lashes defined but not clumpy.

Finish the look with a lick of pinklipstick. Once you've filled in your lips, kissthe back of your hand to blot the lipstickthen, reapply.

Put on your glasses, spritz yourself with perfume and take a look in the mirror.

Yep. Ready to slay.

Get the Look

It's My Party

What do you do when your best friend drags you to a party that you don't want to go to, attended by people who bore you, so she can make out with a boy you don't like? You express your disdain by wearing exactly what you were wearing to school that day.

Attitude: chill

Practical puffer jacket

Practical pants

Practical boots

Barb's Mixtape

Side A

1. Blondie – 'Call Me' (3:32)
2. Pink Floyd – 'Another Brick In The Wall, Pt II' (3:59)
3. The Human League – 'Don't You Want Me' (3:57)
4. Toto – 'Africa' (4:21)
5. David Bowie – 'Let's Dance' (4:08)
6. Eurythmics – 'Sweet Dreams (Are Made Of This)' (3:35)
7. Blondie – 'Heart Of Glass' (3:22)
8. Brotherhood of Man – 'Tie A Yellow Ribbon' (2:55)

Side B

1. David Bowie – 'Ashes To Ashes' (3:35)
2. The Police – 'Don't Stand So Close To Me' (4:02)
3. Soft Cell – 'Tainted Love' (2.41)
4. Modern English – 'I Melt With You' (3:54)
5. Johnny Mandel – 'Suicide Is Painless' (2:53)
6. Psychedelic Furs – 'Love My Way' (3:27)
7. Stealers Wheel – 'Stuck In The Middle With You' (3:23)
8. Kate Bush – 'Babooshka' (3:28)

What's In Barb's Bag?

You can't *be* Barb, but you can accessorise like Barb. And that means being prepared. You want to succeed at school? Watch and learn.

SLEEPERS
A pair of gold sleeper earrings, in case Barb misplaces the ones she's wearing.

CANDY
Because it's important to treat yourself.

GUM
For keeping it fresh.

FRESH
ORIGINAL
BUBBLE GUM

A WATCH
When it's not on Barb's wrist, it's laid out on her desk so she can time herself on her practice exams.

STATIONERY
If you can't handle Barb at her most nerdily prepared, you don't deserve her at her lonely-by-the-swimming-pool vulnerable.

Pinky
INDIANA
29

ERASER
An essential part of the learning process, in Barb's signature colour.

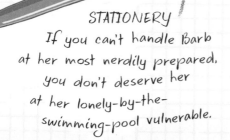

PERFUME

Something sophisticated. Definitely not like the boy-pleasing, mall-hopping, sickly-sweet perfumes the other girls are wearing.

Belle

EXERCISE BOOKS

This one is meticulously filled out with equations and long division, with notes addressed to Nancy in the margins.

TRAPPER KEEPER

The greatest three-ring binder ever created. What's so great about it? Well, the insanely cool rainbow squiggles for starters.

FLASHCARDS

For note-taking, test-prepping and breaking up Barb's debating speech into handy dot-points. A must have for the truly studious student.

Nailed It

Doesn't matter if fashion mags are pushing long, square nails painted power shades of red — this is Hawkins. It's chill.

Here's what Barb and Nancy would pick for a Saturday night manicure sesh.

Spoiler alert: it involves pink.

You'll need

- Nail polish of your choice
- Rubbing alcohol
- Clear basecoat
- Thin paintbrush
- Nail polish remover
- Clear topcoat

Step 1

Pick your colour. Barb and Nancy both gravitate towards pretty, girly shades like light blue, pink and pearl. If you're more of a Barb, you can get a bit more adventurous with navy or plum. If you're more of a Nancy, think about what would impress your crush.

Step 2

To get started, wipe down your nails with rubbing alcohol. This will remove any oil/lotion/hand goop from the surface that could mess up your polish down the track.

Step 3

Do a basecoat. Taking the time to do this will help your manicure last, especially if you're planning on doing something active like a trip into the Upside Down.

Step 4

Now apply your nail colour in neat strokes from the base of each nail to the tip. Paint on two thin coats, then sit and do nothing for a solid 10 minutes. Take this opportunity to gossip about boys or quiz each other on your upcoming trig exam.

Step 5

Dip a thin paintbrush in the nail polish remover and clean up any smudges. This will make your manicure look like it was done in a fancy salon instead of your best friend's bedroom.

Step 6

Once you're a hundred per cent sure the polish is dry, do a topcoat. Wait another ten minutes to ensure that's dry too. The last thing you want to do is ding it up and have to start over.

Step 7

If your mom asks, you're definitely going to take it off before school on Monday. Promise.

CHAPTER THREE

Justice for Barb

TIPS FOR TEENS:

Safe Driving in Hawkins

BROUGHT TO YOU BY THE
Hawkins Police Department

Congratulations on getting your driver's license! You're lucky enough to live in Hawkins, Indiana, one of the safest places in America. But even in our sleepy little town, there are still some dangers you might face when driving. So before you take your car out on the road, please review these safe-driving tips.

1 The most important thing an occupant of any car can do to prevent injury is to *wear a safety belt*. Sure, your mom and dad might not bother wearing them, but recent studies suggest that safety belts are about 57 per cent effective in reducing death or injury in motor vehicle accidents. Establish a car-entry routine that includes putting on a seatbelt — any initial discomfort caused by the belt will quickly fade and you'll get used to wearing it in no time.

2 While we all like a scenic drive through our beautiful town, there are some places that are off-limits to sightseers. *Please avoid the woods around the Hawkins National Laboratory* — the laboratory and its grounds are run by the US Department of Energy, and so it's not accessible to the general public. If you see people in full-body hazmat suits, please leave the area as soon as possible.

3 *Avoid driving while under the influence of alcohol*. Mixing alcohol consumption and driving poses a serious problem for highway safety. A 1978 study showed that a large number of young drivers are involved in serious or fatal crashes even when their blood alcohol level is less than the legal intoxication limit. As a young driver, you are less experienced and more prone to taking risks, so be sure to limit your consumption of alcohol prior to driving. Safety first!

4 We've been experiencing some energy disturbances in Hawkins lately, causing lights to flicker on and off at random. Take care when out on the roads, as these energy outages may affect traffic lights. The folks at the Department of Energy are looking into these issues now and we're confident they'll be resolved in no time.

Have fun out there on the roads! And drive safe.

POLICE DEPARTMENT
HAWKINS INDIANA

MISSING

BARBARA HOLLAND

15 YEARS OLD

LAST SEEN, NOVEMBER 12

Persons Having Any Information Are Requested To Call

Sheriff Jim Hopper - Hawkins Police Dept.
(313)374-1369

Hawkins Police Department	**Runaway Juvenile/Missing Person Report**

Last name: Holland	First name: Barbara	Middle name: N/A					

Alias or nickname: Barb		Sex: Female	Race: Caucasian	D.O.B: 20/09/1966	Place of birth: Indiana	Marital status: Single

Height: 5' 9"	Weight: Unknown	Hair colour: Auburn	Eye colour: Brown	Distinguishing features: Freckles, short hair, wears glasses, bandaid on thumb

Last seen wearing:
Pink knitted sweater, light brown pants, blue puffer jacket, large glasses

Vehicle make: Volkswagen Cabriolet	State: Indiana	License plate number: 30s46T2	Vehicle color: Light blue	Other description: N/A

Person who last saw subject: Nancy Wheeler	Last seen: Harrington residence	Probable cause of absence: Runaway		Probable destination: Unknown

Reporting officer: Officer Callahan	Badge no: 257	Unit no: 10134	Date/time reported: Nov 12, 1983 11:30am	Date/time last seen: Nov 8, 1983 10pm

Narrative: (1) Note the relationship between all listed subjects to missing person. (2) Summarise the circumstances surrounding the disappearance of Subject. (3) Note any suspicious circumstances. (4) Tell complainant to contact Police immediately if Subject is located or contacts family or friends.

On November 12, I was contacted by Mrs Holland, who reported her daughter Barbara was missing after failing to return home after a party at the Harrington residence, thrown by Steve Harrington. Steve and Barbara are both students at Hawkins High School - according to Nancy Wheeler, also a student at Hawkins High School, there was a small party at the Harrington residence on November 8. Nancy and Barbara had an argument. Both Mrs Holland and Nancy are of the opinion that Barbara is missing under suspicious circumstances. Nancy has indicated that she believes something (possibly a bear) 'took' Barbara. However, Barbara's car was discovered by State Police at a bus station, which leads me to believe that she has simply run away. Although she has no history of misbehaviour, it is the opinion of the Department that the townsfolk are on edge after the disappearance of Will Byers, which could go a way to explaining Barbara's actions. We will monitor nearby transit and feel confident that she will turn up soon.

Dear Barb,
I'm sorry if I was a dick to you. I'm not that person anymore. I know Nancy really misses you.
Steve

To Barb,
RIP or whatever.
Tommy H

To Barb,
Who knew you'd ever be this popular? Kidding! It sucks that you're gone.
Send us a postcard from wherever you are (hope it's sunny!).
Love Carol
xox

Dear Barbara,
I never really knew you but you seemed nice.
I saw your mom the other day and she looked so sad.
People must really care about you.
Stay gold,
Laurie

To Barbara,
School just won't be the same without you.
I always saw you hanging out with Nancy and
studying and stuff. I hope you've run away to
somewhere much more fun than Hawkins.
XXX
Becky

Dear Barb,
We love you so much!!!
Luv,
Amy

Hawkins High School
YEARBOOK
Class of '83

Barb –

I'm really sorry for what happened to you.
I feel terrible that I got my brother back
   but you're still gone. I know what it's like in
that place. We think about you every day.
   We won't ever forget you.
   Jonathan

Dear Barb,

There is so much I wish I could say to you. So much that I should have said and didn't. When I think about the last time I saw you, my heart breaks into a million tiny pieces. I know you were trying to look after me. You were trying to be my guardian just like I asked you to be, but I was too busy thinking about myself. I didn't listen.

I'm sorry for staying with Steve instead of leaving the party with you that night. Maybe if I'd left, things would have turned out differently. Maybe you'd still be here. (Please don't be mad at Steve though. I know you don't think much of him, but everything he's done for me ... I think you'd be proud of how he's changed.) I'm sorry for putting my feelings for Steve first. I'm sorry for being so selfish.

I wish I could call you up and talk about what happened at school, or what we want to do on the weekend, or how annoying my kid brother is, or all the things we're going to do when we're grown up. I wish that I could walk into class tomorrow and see you sitting at your desk. I miss you so much.

Barb, you're my best friend. You'll always be my best friend. You were the best friend anyone could ever want. I didn't tell you this enough and I took you for granted but ... I love you. And I won't ever forget you.

Love,
Nancy
xox

PS. I'm not giving up hope that somehow you'll come back to me.

Smith Street Books

Published in 2017 by Smith Street Books
Melbourne | Australia
smithstreetbooks.com

ISBN: 978-1-925418-47-7

The moral right of the author have been asserted.
CIP data is available from the National Library of Australia.

Publisher: Paul McNally
Author: Nadia Bailey
Project editor: Hannah Koelmeyer
Design: Stephanie Spartels
Illustration: Phil Constantinesco (Faunesque), The Illustration Room
Images on pages 14, 15, 32, 33, 44 and 45 from stock.adobe.com

Printed & bound in China by C&C Offset Printing Co., Ltd.

Book 33
10 9 8 7 6 5 4 3 2 1

Please note: This title is not affiliated in any way to the Netflix series Stranger Things. We are just big fans. Please don't sue us.